Everything You Need to Know About

GRIEVING

Grieving can cause strong feelings of sadness.

Everything You Need To Know About
GRIEVING

Karen Spies

THE ROSEN PUBLISHING GROUP, INC.
NEW YORK

Published in 1990, 1993, 1997 by The Rosen Publishing Group, Inc.
29 East 21st Street, New York, New York 10010

Revised Edition 1997

Manufactured in the United States of America.

Library of Congress Cataloging-in-Publication Data

Spies, Karen Bornemann.
    Everything you need to know about grieving / Karen Spies.
    (The need to know library)
    Includes bibliographical references and index.
    ISBN 0-8239-2623-0
    1. Bereavement—Psychological aspects—Juvenile literature. 2. Loss
(Psychology)—Juvenile literature. I. Title. II. Series.
BF575.G7S65 1990
155.9'37—dc20   90-36541
                                                             CIP
                                                             AC

Contents

Introduction 6

1. What Is the "Right Way" To Grieve? 9

2. Working Through Grief 15

3. Talking About Death 21

4. A Death in the Family 29

5. When A Parent Dies 33

6. She Was Too Young To Die 41

7. I Didn't Get To Say Good-bye 45

8. What Happens After a Death? 49

9. Recovering from Grief 55

Glossary—*Explaining New Words* 60

Where to Go for Help 61

For Further Reading 62

Index 63

Introduction

Grief is a feeling of deep sadness caused by an important loss or change in your life. You grieve when you lose someone you love or something that is important to you—whether it is a parent, a brother or sister, a friend, or a pet. While the most painful losses often result from the death of a loved one, people also grieve when they experience misfortune. This can happen when parents divorce or a best friend moves far away.

Everyone experiences loss at some time. When a loved one dies, you experience many different feelings. These feelings may include shock, disbelief, numbness, anger, depression, embarrassment, and guilt. Whether you experience some or all of these emotions depends on your unique situation. Each person experiences death and loss in a different way.

Grieving for the first time can make you wonder how you should behave. You may ask yourself, "Is it okay to cry?" "Who can I talk to?" "Why don't I feel anything?" "How long am I going to feel this way?" If you know someone else who is grieving, you may wonder how you should act toward him or her. All these difficult questions will be discussed in this book.

There is no right or wrong way to grieve. But there are some ways that may help you through the grieving process. For example, it is helpful to let out your feelings, no matter how sad or hurt you feel. Death and loss are not easy subjects to talk about, but sharing your feelings with someone you love and trust will help ease the pain.

You will also need to take care of yourself in order to recover from the loss. It's easy to forget that you need to eat well, get enough sleep, and enjoy life again after someone you love has died.

Remember that your grief will decrease over time. While there is no time limit for grief, you will begin to feel better one day. You may get upset from time to time, but the overwhelming feelings that come directly after a loss will gradually fade.

Once you understand the grieving process, you will be more prepared to cope with the confusion and pain that come when you lose someone you love.

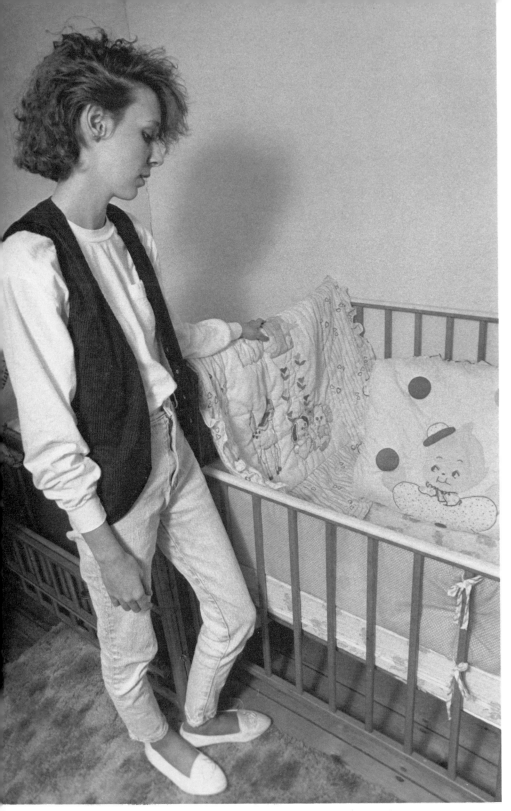

Losing a loved member of the family is a great shock.

Chapter 1

What Is the "Right Way" To Grieve?

Grief happens when you experience an important loss. Loss means change, and change can be very difficult. The death of a family member is, of course, a great loss. But you might also grieve over other things. The death of a pet, for example, or breaking up with a boyfriend or girlfriend could also make you feel empty and sad.

People experience grief in different ways. There is no "right way" to grieve. Consider these stories about three young people who experienced grief. Notice the different feelings they had.

Marta and her family went away for the weekend. They left their cat, Tiger, alone in the house. Marta made sure to leave enough food and water for him.

The night Marta returned home, Tiger was sick. He had knocked over his water bowl and had run out of water. Marta stayed up all night with him. In the morning, while Marta was sleeping, her parents took Tiger to the veterinarian (animal doctor). The vet had to put him to sleep.

When Marta found out that Tiger was dead, she was very upset. She was angry at her parents for taking him to the vet without her. Why didn't they wake her up? Why did they let the vet put Tiger to sleep? She never had a chance to say good-bye.

Cindy's Aunt Julie was her mother's sister. The day the family got the news that Aunt Julie died of cancer, Cindy's mother couldn't stop crying. Cindy didn't know what to say to her. She had a few nice memories of her aunt. But Cindy felt like she didn't really know Aunt Julie very well because she lived far away from her aunt and hardly ever got a chance to visit her. Cindy was only eight years old the last time she saw Aunt Julie. Now she is fifteen.

Cindy felt bad that Aunt Julie had died, especially since her mom missed her so much. But Cindy felt like she herself wasn't sad enough. Sometimes this made her feel guilty. She was afraid her mother would be upset with her for not being sad enough.

Darryl couldn't believe this was happening. His best friend Pete had been killed in a car accident the night before. The worst part was that Pete had been driving home from Darryl's house when it happened.

At first, all Darryl could feel was shock. "I can't believe it," he said to himself over and over again. But when the shock started to wear off, Darryl thought of something else.

When Pete left the house the night before, it was raining pretty hard. He pulled out of Darryl's driveway much too fast. Then he skidded on the wet pavement. Darryl stood on the front porch and watched, laughing the whole time. Why hadn't he yelled at Pete to slow down? Darryl kept asking himself this question. "If I hadn't just laughed at him, Pete might still be alive," he thought. "Maybe I could have kept this from happening."

These three young people experienced grief in different ways. They all felt sad. But each one also had other feelings that they had to deal with.

Here are some of the feelings people have when they are grieving:

Shock

Often, people are shocked when they first learn about a death. It is especially difficult when the death is totally unexpected. The family has no time to prepare for their loss. Like Darryl, they may find it hard to believe that someone they care about is dead.

Sadness and Longing

Sadness is probably the most common feeling of grief. When a person or a pet has died, your life changes. Change is hard to accept. Darryl couldn't imagine life without his best friend, Pete. No one could ever replace him.

It's common to miss or long for the person who has died. It's difficult to accept that he or she is gone and will no longer be an active part of your life.

Anger

You may be angry at the person who has died. You may feel abandoned. If your loved one died in an accident, you may be mad at him for his carelessness.

You may also be angry at the people around you. You may feel that they didn't do enough to help. Marta was angry at her parents and blamed them for Tiger's death.

It's okay to feel angry, as long as you don't keep this feeling bottled up. To release your anger, try playing a sport you enjoy or consider writing about your frustration in a journal.

Guilt

Cindy felt guilty about not being sadder when her aunt died. Darryl felt guilty about not telling Pete to drive more carefully. Cindy and Darryl did nothing wrong. But guilt is another natural part of grieving. Like anger, it usually fades in time.

Fear

Death is scary. If it is sudden, it can make you feel uncertain about your own future. You may feel like everything can be taken away without any notice. You may even start to think about your own death. You also feel like you have no control over the death of a loved one and the changes that it brings. Darryl tried to regain some control by taking responsibility for Pete's accident. But Darryl had nothing to do with Pete's death. It's frightening to think that you can't always prevent a loved one from dying.

You may also begin to isolate yourself from other people. You may be afraid to get close to anyone because you don't want to lose another person and experience the same kind of pain. But it's important to be around people who love and support you.

Depression

When sadness goes on for a long time, it can become depression. Other feelings, like anger and guilt, can also cause depression. When people are depressed, they have very little energy or interest in life. It is important to deal with all your feelings when you grieve. Otherwise, they might lead to depression.

Each person reacts in his or her own way to loss and death. There is no one way or correct way to grieve.

If you lose someone or something special in your life, you may feel many different ways. It is important to talk to someone about your feelings. Other people can provide the understanding and support you need to get through the grieving process.

The loss of a pet is painful. Sometimes having the chance to say good-bye can make parting easier.

Chapter 2

Working Through Grief

*J*eff's dog, Buster, always met him at the door when Jeff came home from school. They played catch with a ball. Buster never tired of the game. Then Buster got sick. He stayed in his dog bed for most of the day. Jeff could tell it was hard for Buster to move.

One day, when Jeff was at school, Buster died in his sleep. Jeff's mom took Buster to the veterinarian. She didn't want Jeff to see Buster's body.

Jeff cried when he found out that Buster was dead. He was angry, too. He felt that he missed the chance to say good-bye to his pet. Jeff was surprised at his strong feelings.

Jeff's mom patted him on the shoulder. "Don't feel so bad, Jeff. I know you miss Buster, but we can get a new dog."

"I don't want a new dog," Jeff yelled. He ran to his bedroom and slammed the door.

Jeff is upset. His life has changed suddenly. Jeff misses his pet. He has powerful feelings, and he is not sure how to handle them.

Nina and Jaleh were best friends. They played softball for their high school. Nina was the pitcher, Jaleh covered first base. Together, they helped their team make the play-offs.

Two weeks before the play-offs, Jaleh arrived at practice very upset. When Nina asked her what was wrong, she started crying and said that her mom got a new job and her family was moving away. Nina was stunned.

"Moving? I don't believe it! What are we going to do?"

"It's awful. We're moving in a week! I won't even get to play in the championship," said Jaleh.

When Jaleh moved, Nina became depressed. That week, she didn't want to go to school and she didn't want to go to softball practice. She didn't even care if the team won the championship or not.

Nina feels sad and alone. She's worried she won't play well in the championship without Jaleh. And she thinks it's not worthwhile to try to win if she can't share the experience with her best friend.

Kim used to have lots of friends. She had a steady boyfriend named Yoshi. Her grades were good. Kim was happy with her life. Then her parents got a divorce. Her father moved out of the house. Her mother had to work longer hours to make ends meet. Kim had to do most of the household chores. She couldn't go out with Yoshi as often. When her friends had fun, Kim got angry. When they called her, she didn't feel like talking. After a while, they stopped calling.

Kim is really upset, but it seems like no one understands her problems. She misses her father. She is angry that she has so little time to spend with friends. Kim wonders if she will ever feel happy again.

I Don't Deserve This

You may not understand why bad things happen to you. Jeff did nothing wrong. Death is not a punishment. Buster died because he was very old. Nina didn't understand why her best friend had to move away. She felt it was pointless to be a good student or a good pitcher if life was going to fall apart anyway. Kim could not stop her parents' divorce.

Like these teens, you may feel helpless in your grief. There are times when you can't predict or prevent loss and death. There are no easy answers to your pain and suffering. But you can begin to heal by facing your feelings. This is called "grief work."

Facing and letting out your feelings will help you through the grieving process and allow you to move on

Disbelief is often the first reaction when you hear about a death.

with your life. It's not an easy thing to do. But keeping your feelings inside makes it harder to ease your pain. Let's look at what Jeff, Nina, and Kim did to handle their grief.

Jeff wrote his mother a note about what was bothering him. She was glad Jeff told her how he felt. They cried together about Buster and hugged each other. They decided to get another pet later, when they both were ready.

Nina went to talk with her coach. She told her how she felt now that Jaleh was gone. The coach listened to Nina. Then she suggested that Nina talk to the other players on the team. Together, they decided to try to win the championship for Jaleh. Nina realized that Jaleh wanted her to play even though she couldn't be there. Nina felt better after talking out her feelings. She was excited again about the game.

Kim asked her mom about the divorce. She found out there were many reasons for it. Both of her parents told Kim how much they loved her. They both found ways to spend more time with Kim. They hired a college student to help Kim with her schoolwork. They gave Kim fewer chores, so she had more time to go out with Yoshi again. Kim called a friend, and soon other friends began to call her again.

Feeling Better

Grief can feel unbearable at times. You will need time away from grieving. Try to find healthy ways to distract yourself. Listening to music or exercising can help you to release the pressure. Some find it comforting to write down their thoughts and feelings. It may take time to find out what works best for you.

You may be tempted to use alcohol or other drugs to forget your problems. Taking a drug is not a healthy way to deal with grief. Drugs only add to your problems and make it more difficult to cope with your pain. If you feel lost or find yourself turning to drugs, talk to someone you trust. Be sure to get the help you need.

It takes time to work out your grief.

Chapter 3

Talking About Death

*J*uan's grandmother had been ill with cancer for a long time. She was in the hospital. One day, Juan's mother told him, "Your grandma is no longer in pain. She is now resting in peace."

It is difficult to face death even though it is a fact of life. Sometimes it is even hard to say the word "death." People often use other words to communicate the idea of death. They may say that the deceased has "passed away," "is lost," or has "passed on." These words may make it easier to accept the painful reality of death. They are also more gentle when speaking to someone about the loss of a loved one. A person may not be emotionally prepared to hear you say "How are you taking the death of your father?" But she may be more comfortable if you say, "I'm sorry to hear that your father has passed away. Is there anything I can do?" Talking about death in a sensitive way can make it seem less scary. It helps you get through the grieving process.

What Is Death?

When a person dies, his or her breathing and heart stop. The deceased cannot think or feel pain. The person cannot see or hear. Once someone dies, he or she will never come back again.

Death used to be more common in everyday life than it is today. Lack of medical knowledge and poor hygiene led to the spread of many deadly diseases that today can easily be prevented or cured. People who became sick often died, sometimes at a very young age. Many people died at home in their beds. Their families grieved over the loss, but accepted it as a natural part of life.

As cures and treatments were discovered for many diseases, death gradually became more removed from daily life. Today, many people have trouble accepting death and don't want to talk or even think about it. But talking about your feelings and fears is important. It helps you gain perspective on your loss and work through your pain. Also, the people you talk to can offer emotional support and helpful insights based on their own experiences.

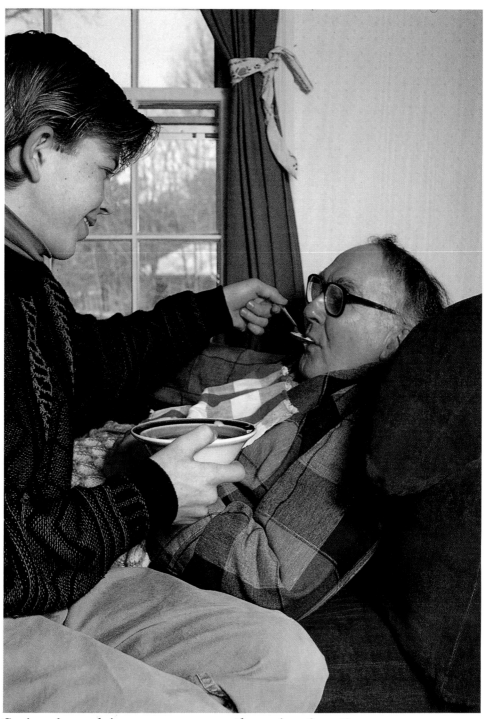

Caring for a dying person eases the pain of parting.

When Darin's father died, his aunt came over to the house. She put her arm around Darin. "Your dad in gone now. You must be brave, because you're the man of the house now."

Darin didn't feel brave. He felt alone. He wanted to cry, but he didn't think he should. That wouldn't be brave.

Darin's aunt loved him. She wanted to be helpful, so she said what she thought was right. But what she said put a lot of pressure on Darin and kept him from expressing his grief. Darin needed to let his feelings out. He felt hurt, and he needed to cry.

Many Reasons

There are many reasons why people and animals die. Many people die when they are old. Some people die of illnesses. Others die in accidents or wars. Sometimes people are murdered by other people.

Death is part of the cycle of life. All living things, such as plants and animals, experience birth and death. When a plant dies, it makes room for a new plant to grow. It is the same with people. If no one ever died, there wouldn't be any room for new people to be born. There would be no land left to live on and not enough food to eat.

You may now have a pet, or you may plan to get one someday. You will love your pet, and take good care of it. You may feel as close to your pet as you do to a human friend. But pets, just like people, must

It is important to discuss your feelings with another person.

die. When this happens, you will be sad and upset.
You may experience many of the same feelings
people have when a loved one dies. Losing a pet may
be your first experience with death. As painful as
this loss can be, it may help you face your fear of
death.

*Berta's grandfather died when she was ten years
old. Her parents went to the funeral, but they made
Berta stay home alone. Berta still remembers sitting
in her room by herself. She loved her grandfather.
She looked out the window and wondered what to do.
She was crying, and she wanted someone to hug her.*

Berta's grandfather was the only person she knew who had ever died. She missed him. And she was afraid. What if one of her parents died? What would she do?

Berta really needed to be comforted by her mom and dad. She needed them to remind her that they were both strong and healthy. She needed them to tell her that she should not be afraid.

When someone you love dies, you need to express your feelings. Tell your mom or dad if you want to cry. Let them know you need to be hugged. Hug them, too. If you show your feelings, you may help your parents express their emotions, too.

Knowing What to Expect

Knowing what kind of changes a dying person goes through may help you to prepare for his or her death. People who are dying may look very different than they once did. They may lose a lot of weight, or parts of their body may become swollen. Sometimes a dying person's hair changes color or falls out.

You may find it hard to talk to someone who is dying of an illness. You may feel uncomfortable, because you are not used to seeing the person the way he or she looks now. Remember that the person has not changed. He or she is the same person you have always known. Be ready to listen. Try to talk to the person the way you have in the past.

Dying at Home

If a loved one is dying at home, you will face many changes. Whoever is taking care of the person will have less time to spend with you. You may not be able to have friends over as often. Everyone will probably be more tired.

If this happens in your home, try to be understanding. Help to care for the patient. Stop in and talk to him or her about what you do during the day.

What Is a Hospice?

Sometimes a dying person goes to a hospice. A hospice is a nursing home for people who are dying. The people who work there can help your whole family. They are trained to help people face their fear of death.

If someone you know is dying, talking about your feelings will help you deal with what is happening. Ask your parents any questions you have or talk to another trusted adult. A religious leader may be a good person to speak with because he or she can offer you support and guidance. Religious leaders also can help you understand death in the context of your religious faith.

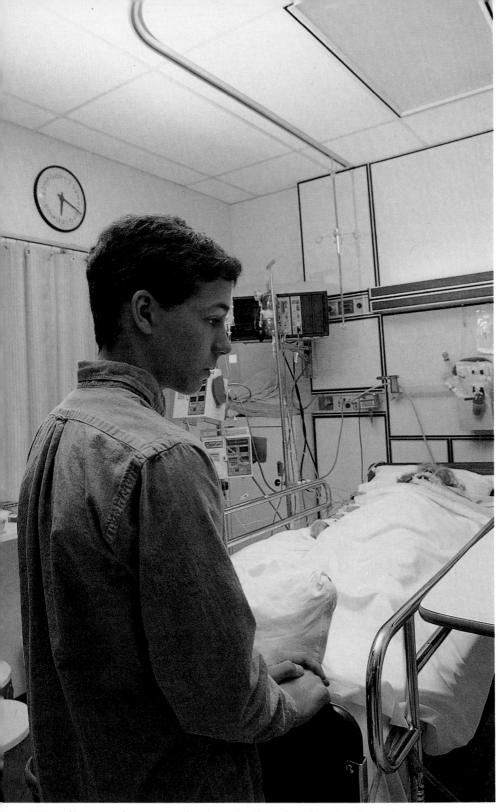

We all must learn to deal with the death of a loved one.

Chapter 4

A Death in the Family

Steve's Uncle Cal felt more like an older brother than an uncle. He was only seven years older than Steve. So when Steve learned that Cal was dying of AIDS, he was shocked. A few months later, Cal died. Steve felt angry that there was no cure to help his uncle. When he died, it was like losing a good friend.

Each year in the summer, Natalie went with her mother and brothers to see her grandfather. He lived on a farm in North Carolina. But this summer will be different. This year her grandfather died in February. Natalie's mother went to the funeral by herself. She didn't want Natalie and her brothers to miss any school. This made Natalie sad. She wishes she could have said goodbye to her grandfather. She wonders what this summer will be like without him.

Ben's father's cousin, Anna, was in the hospital for many months. Everyone knew she was dying. Sometimes Ben went with his dad to visit Anna. Ben never knew what to say to her. She always seemed glad to see him. But she was too weak from the pain to talk. When she died, Ben felt relieved. She had been sick for such a long time. Still, he felt guilty for being relieved. He wanted to help his father feel better, but he wasn't sure how. At the funeral he reached over to take his dad's hand. It must have been the right thing to do. His dad squeezed his hand and kept holding on to it.

Steve, Natalie, and Ben all had family members who died. One day someone in your family will die, too. Maybe someone already has. You may have a number of different feelings when this happens.

You probably will be very sad. You might feel sorry, like Natalie, that you didn't get to say good-bye. You might also be curious about the future, like Natalie. Or, like Steve, you might feel angry about losing someone you love.

When someone has been very sick for a long time, it can feel like a relief for that person to die. This is especially true when the sick person has been suffering. Ben felt guilty about being relieved when Anna died. But there was no reason to feel guilty. His reaction was very normal. He was sorry Anna died. But he was glad that her illness and pain were finally over.

The company of friends can help during the grieving process.

It's often hard to know what to say to someone who is dying. It's also hard to know what to say to the family and friends of someone who has died.

If you aren't sure what to say, it's all right to be quiet. People will usually understand that it's difficult to express your feelings. Sometimes you can reach out to people in other ways. You might take someone's hand, or give someone a hug. Perhaps just by being there to listen to the grieving person is all the comfort they need.

One day you may grieve over a death or a loss. When that happens, try to remember that *other* people may not know what to say to *you*. These people will want you to know that they care. At times you may feel like you just want to be left alone. Friends and family should understand that, too. But try to talk about your grief with someone you trust when you do feel ready.

Chapter 5

When A Parent Dies

Most kids worry at some time or other that one or both of their parents might die. Almost everyone has had this feeling. Luckily, most kids' parents do not die when the kids are young. But some do. If this happens to you, it is hard to believe. You may feel as if the world has come to an end. You may wish your life was over too. You will probably feel sorry for yourself. These are all normal feelings. Janna had many of them.

Janna's father was hit by a car when he crossed the street. At first she felt numb. How could this be happening to her? She thought bad things only happened to other people.

Janna began to worry a lot. She didn't feel like eating. She couldn't sleep very well at night because she often dreamed about her dad. She dreamed that he came to talk to her.

Then Janna was afraid. What if her mother died? What if something happened to her brother?

If your parent has just died, you may feel like Janna. You can't think much about the future. You feel as if you are living in a bad dream. If only you could wake up; then the terrible sadness would go away.

People have these feelings even when they know ahead of time that someone is dying. If a loved one has been sick for a long time, you might expect to be prepared to cope with his or her death. But even this kind of death is a shock. You cannot really prepare yourself for the death of someone you love.

People are the only living beings who know that they will die someday. Despite this knowledge, it is still hard to understand death. How could your parent die? How could this special person not be an active part of your life anymore?

This feeling is called disbelief. It protects you from experiencing pain by making you feel numb. While disbelief is a natural reaction to death, it's important to accept the death of a loved one in order to begin the healing process.

If a parent dies, new responsibilities have to be accepted by other members of the family.

As time passes, you begin to miss the dead person very much. At first, you may be able to see your dead parent very clearly. You remember the smell of your mom's perfume, or your dad's shaving cream. You wish your mother or father could be there to hold you.

You may dream about your dead parent, like Janna did. Some kids find this a comfort. The dead person seems near to them again. In their dreams, they can feel happy.

As time goes by, your memories may fade in and out. Sometimes it will seem that the person is in the room with you. Other times you will not be able to remember the sound of the person's voice.

On some days, no matter how hard you try you will not be able to remember the dead person. This is scary. But it seems to be a normal part of grieving. Your mind and body are beginning to accept the death. Something inside of you is getting ready to let go of the parent.

Once you can let go, and accept the death, your memories come back. Now they seem to be memories about good feelings and happy times together. You will remember things like your mom's favorite joke, or the way your dad sang in the shower.

Little by little, you begin to understand that your parent is never coming back. Sometimes it can take many months or even years before a person can come to terms with the death of a parent. You may cry harder at this time than when you first found out about the death. That's okay. You may also feel scared. You wonder what will happen to you. Who will take care of you from now on? Along with these worries you may feel jealousy, anger, or guilt. Shawn, Amanda, and Greg had these feelings.

Shawn's father died when Shawn was fifteen. Shawn said, "My dad died just when I was getting to know him. He didn't get to see my first touchdown. I know he would have been proud of me. I felt like his death cut off the beginning of a new relationship with my dad. I never got the chance to know him as I got older."

Shawn felt cheated. When he saw other boys with their fathers, he was jealous. These are normal feelings.

Amanda and her mother had a big fight one morning about her curfew. Amanda had come in late the night before and her mother grounded her for two weeks. Amanda stormed up to her room and slammed the door. She wrote in her diary that she hated her mother.

Two days later, Amanda's mother was killed in a car accident on her way home from work. Amanda was in shock. She was angry at herself for fighting with her

*mother over something so petty. She went upstairs
and tore up her diary.*

Arguments are a normal part of life. It's not
realistic to expect to get along with your family and
friends all of the time. Never fighting with someone
won't prevent him or her from dying.

Amanda knew that she did not cause her mother's
death. But she still felt guilty. In time, Amanda will
learn to cope with her guilt and understand that
anger is a natural emotion.

*Greg's dad died of a heart attack. Greg's mom
had to go back to work. Sometimes she said things like
"Why did your dad leave me like this? I just can't
make it alone." Greg was scared when his mom talked
that way.*

Greg's mom did not mean what she said. Her
angry words came out of the great pain she felt. She
reassured Greg that she loved him, and that she
wouldn't leave him.

Janna, Shawn, Amanda, and Greg had many
normal feelings of grief. They felt sadness, shock,
anger, worry, guilt, and fear. Facing these feelings
and dealing with them is part of grieving. With time,
you will be able to let these feelings go.

Another part of grieving is adjusting to the changes
in your life. You will face many changes when a

parent dies. You may have to live in a new place. You may have to help out more at home. Your other parent may have to work more each week to earn enough money to support the family. If you are old enough, you might need to get a part-time job to help out, too.

Give yourself time to face these changes. You will feel sadness for a long time. But after many months, you will probably feel less pain.

Be patient during the time that your family is trying to decide what to do next. Try to make the best of each day. Share with others the things that bother you. Together you can face this difficult time.

When you lose a loved one, keeping good memories alive helps.

Expressing your feelings is important in accepting a death.

Chapter 6

She Was Too Young To Die

*T*eena's sister Carrie died from taking drugs. Teena said, "How can I go out with my friends and laugh and have fun? I'm hurting too much. I can't believe that Carrie is gone. I feel so angry. She was so young."

Dawn and Conrad were together for three years when Dawn was diagnosed with meningitis. She died one week later. Conrad couldn't believe it. He had been with her for so long and now she was gone. "It happened so fast. One day we were planning prom night and the next week, she was in the hospital. It doesn't make any sense. She was so healthy. Anyone can get sick. I'm scared it will happen to me, too."

Peter's baby brother died. "We never got to take Bobby home from the hospital. It seems so unfair. Bobby never got a chance to do anything," said Peter.

It can be especially hard to accept the death of a young person. When you're young, you usually don't think about death. You have your whole life ahead of you. You may think young people aren't supposed to die.

Sometimes there are no clear answers to why some people get sick. For this reason, you may feel confused and angry when a young person dies. You may also start to worry about your own death. Conrad saw his girlfriend become sick without warning. He thought the same could happen to him. When a loved one dies, it does not increase your chances of dying, too.

Twelve-year-old Laura cannot imagine what this Christmas will be like without her four-year-old sister, Trisha. Trisha died of a brain tumor. The whole family had delighted in Trisha's joy at Christmas.

Kevin's best friend, Joey, died of cancer. They had gone to camp together every summer. They had walked to school together every day for seven years. Kevin will be starting junior high in September. He feels sad when he thinks about walking to school every day without Joey.

Perhaps the most difficult loss you may have to deal with as a young person is the death of a sibling or a friend. Many people in our lives live long and healthy lives. But sometimes death comes to someone young. This kind of death may seem even greater than the death of an adult. We grieve for the things a young person didn't get to do, or to be. We grieve because we will miss a friend or sibling we expected to grow up with. We realize how many things they will never be able to share with us. We will miss them at family celebrations, and very special occasions.

Your grief may make it hard to keep up in school. You may find that you forget things easily. The other kids may seem happy and busy. This might make you angry. All this is a normal part of grieving. Be patient. After a while you won't feel quite so down. You will be able to keep your mind on other things.

Even after you get over feeling anger, pain, and loss every time you think about your sibling or friend, it will take a long time to heal. Remembering things you shared will hurt a lot in the beginning. Your pain may last a long time. You will always have memories. But after time has passed, the pain will lessen.

Some kids find that talking with friends is helpful. Others like to write down their thoughts. Drawing pictures about feelings may also help to ease your pain.

Death is never easy to understand. The death of a young person is especially hard. No one knows why some people live and others die.

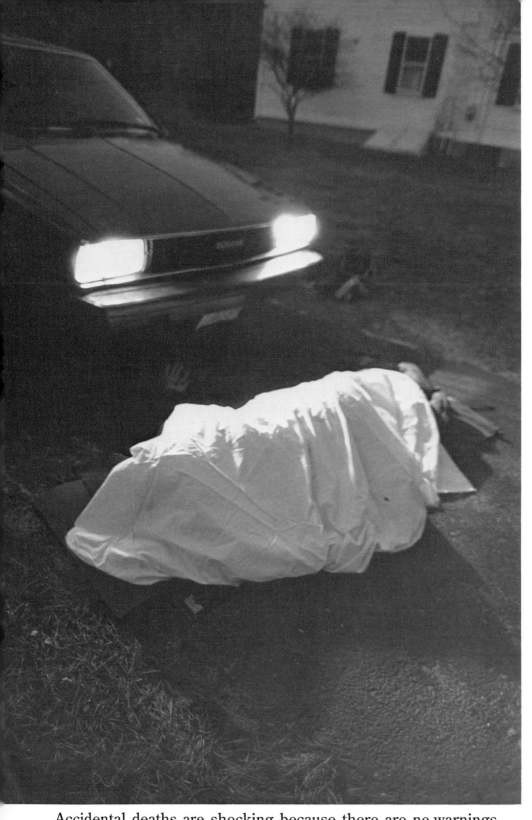

Accidental deaths are shocking because there are no warnings.

Chapter 7

I Didn't Get to Say Good-bye

*S*eth's sister died in a boating accident. Seth *and his family were shocked and numb. Joy was only seventeen. She had looked forward to the boat trip for many months. Now she was dead.*

Seth dreamed that he could have saved Joy. He was supposed to go on the trip, too, but he had gotten sick. "If only I had been there," Seth thought. "I am a great swimmer. I could have helped Joy."

Death Without Warning

Joy died by accident. Accidental deaths are very shocking, because they happen without notice. You have no way to prepare for such a death. There is usually very little you could do to keep such a death from happening.

Sudden deaths often cause many guilt feelings. Seth wondered, "Could I have helped my sister? Did she suffer?

A good way to face guilt is to say out loud, "I feel guilty. I wish I had done something different." As soon as you name what you are feeling, it will be easier for you to face it.

You may feel like screaming, or crying loudly, when you think about this kind of a death. It is normal to have these feelings. Be sure to tell a parent or another adult what is bothering you. Then they will not worry about you when you show such strong feelings.

Remember that each person has his or her own way to grieve. Playing a hard game of tennis may make you feel better. Talking with a good friend may help. Find what works for you. Doing things that make you feel better will help you to deal with your fears. You will grow stronger inside. Then it will be easier for you to face death.

Kareem was eighteen. He had finished high school, but he was still living with his parents. Each time Kareem started a new job, he quit after a few months. He wasn't able to make many friends.

Kareem had tried to commit suicide (kill himself) two times. He had already planned his funeral service.

Kareem's mother thought he would feel better if he lived in his own place. Kareem pretended to be happy about moving, but inside he was afraid.

On the night he moved, Kareem took many sleeping pills and died. His mother blamed herself for Kareem's death.

Suicide

When someone commits suicide, that person's family and friends may feel guilty. Like Kareem's mother, people who are close to suicide victims may feel like they have failed in some way. They may believe that they should have been able to make the person want to live.

According to the U.S. Department of Health and Human Services, about 5,000 teenagers committed suicide in 1994. Although there are no official U.S. statistics on attempted suicide, the American Association of Suicidology estimates that there are about 25 attempts for each death by suicide.

The first question most people ask about teen suicide is why? Often, people who commit suicide feel depressed, lonely, and unloved. They may feel like they have failed to live up to their own expectations or the expectations of others. Death may come to be seen as the only way to escape their pain.

Teens who try to kill themselves may be having trouble in school, at home, or with drugs. Some of these young people think no one cares if they live or die. Some say things like, "Everyone would be better off without me." Teens who kill themselves may not think about how their sudden deaths would affect others.

Kids who think about killing themselves often show signs of how they feel. They are depressed (they feel very down, very sad). They may talk about wanting to die. They may give away their favorite things. This is part of their way of getting ready to die. Often, they refuse to talk to family members about their feelings.

If anyone you know talks or acts this way, get help. Tell your parents or another adult you trust. Look in the back of this book for places to call for help.

If you ever feel so depressed that you think you want to die, tell someone right away. Don't let the hopeless feelings grow.

Other Sudden Deaths

Sometimes young people die in violent ways. They are killed by another person, or they die in a war. These kinds of deaths do not happen often. They may be the hardest kinds of deaths to face, because they seem so unfair.

No one likes to talk about sudden death. Accidents, suicide, wars, and murder are hard to think about. They seem to be such a waste of life. But these kinds of death must be faced, too. The most important thing to remember is this: You are not alone, no matter how bad life may seem. You can find comfort. After a time of grieving your life will start to feel normal again.

Chapter 8

What Happens After a Death?

*W*hen Steve was fourteen and Tara was eight,
their uncle died. Steve's parents talked to their pas-
tor about the funeral. "Steve and Tara loved their
uncle so much. They are too young to go to the fu-
neral, aren't they? They may become upset if they see
their uncle's body."

The pastor said, "Ask Steve and Tara what they
want to do. The funeral is an important time. It
gives everyone a chance to share in the service for the
dead person. It's a good way to honor the life of the
person who died."

Parents sometimes want to protect their chil-
dren from the sadness of death. Steve and Tara's
parents wanted to keep them away from their
uncle's funeral. But their pastor reminded them
that the funeral was very important. It could help
Steve and Tara accept their uncle's death.

The Process of Mourning

Funerals and memorial services are part of the process of *mourning*. Mourning refers to the ways people show their grief when someone has died. In the past, people often wore black clothing for a year or more to show they were in mourning. Some people still do this.

There are many ways to mourn. One of the most common ways is the funeral. Funerals let friends and family members of the person who has died come together to share their grief. They allow people to find comfort in their religious beliefs. They let people show their love and respect for the person who has died. They also give people the chance to say good-bye.

Before the funeral, the body of the dead person is taken to a funeral home. That is a special place where people can go to visit with the dead person's family. The body is dressed and laid out in a casket. The casket (also called a "coffin") is the box or chest used to bury the body. Most often the casket is kept in a special room at a funeral home. Visiting hours are set. People who knew the dead person can come to comfort the living members of the family. Sometimes the casket is open, so people can view the body. It is helpful for some people who are grieving to be able to see the dead person one more time.

You may worry about looking at the body. Remember that the body is still part of the person you

Neighbors and friends can comfort grieving families.

loved. But do not feel ashamed if you decide not to view the body. Many people prefer to preserve a living image of the loved one.

Different cultures have different funeral customs. Some people have a *wake* before a funeral. This is a time when people get together in special rooms in funeral homes to remember someone who has died.

Many funerals are held at a funeral home, church, or synagogue. Often a religious leader will speak about the person who has died. He or she might read from the Bible or other holy books, and lead people in prayers. Sometimes friends or family members of the deceased also speak.

People visit grieving Jewish families *after* a funeral. Many Jewish families observe a mourning period, called a *shiva,* that lasts for several days. During that time family members express their sadness, and friends come to comfort them. After the shiva, the family resumes its normal activities.

Making Choices

Many times family members will know in advance the arrangements that the dead person requested. They may have talked about it or even written it down. Some people may wish to be buried in a cemetery. They may own a *cemetery plot* many years before their death. Other people may wish to be *cremated* after they die. Cremation changes the body to ashes by burning. The ashes are clean and white. Ashes may be stored in a small jar or *urn*. Sometimes they are buried or spread over some place that was special to the person who died.

Showing That You Care

There are many ways to show sympathy to the dead person's family. Some people send cards, special notes, or flowers. Others choose to donate money in memory of the dead person. The money may be sent to an organization or charity that the dead person supported in his or her lifetime.

The family of the dead person may also need some help at first. They are probably still in shock. Many people bring food. They offer to help with tasks such as cleaning or shopping.

Another important way to help is by listening and talking to the person who is grieving. Both visits and telephone calls are helpful. Perhaps you know someone who is mourning. Think about what you would like if you were grieving. This will help you know what to do and say.

When you are grieving, don't be afraid to share your feelings. Someone may ask, "How are you?" You may answer, "I'm fine." This is how you want to feel. This is probably what the other person wants to hear. But deep inside, you may not feel fine. Then you should say something such as, "I really feel down today. I need to be with someone. Could you come over for a while?"

Getting back into social activities helps the recovery process.

Chapter 9

Recovering from Grief

The time that it takes to recover from grief varies from person to person. Your grief cannot be hurried. Doctors say that grief over the death of a loved one can last as long as two years. Recovering from other kinds of grief may not take as long. Slowly, you learn to accept your loss and to live with your feelings. The intense feelings of grief eventually fade, although your sadness may never completely go away.

As your life returns to normal, you may face more changes. That is what happened to Ronnie and Justine.

Ronnie is thirteen. He used to live in a big house with his parents and his sister, Rochelle. One summer, Ronnie's mom became sick and went to the hospital. She died from breast cancer in the fall.

Raising two kids alone was hard for Ronnie's dad. He struggled to pay for the medical bills. Within a year, Ronnie's father decided to sell the house. It was too big and expensive. Ronnie was just starting to adjust to the loss of his mother. Now they had to move, too. "I feel like I'm losing my mom all over again. This is her house. I know that it will be easier on my dad, but sometimes I just feel so bad that I don't know what to do."

Justine's dad died last year. Recently, her mom has started to go out on dates. Lately, she has brought Max home quite a few times. Max is divorced. He has two girls of his own. Justine wonders what will happen if her mom and Max get married. Will she have to move? What if she has to share a room with one of Max's girls?

"I was just getting used to Dad being gone," Justine said. "My life was beginning to settle down. Now it looks like it's going to be messed up again."

The death of a family member can bring many disruptive changes to your life. This only makes it harder to cope with the pain of losing a loved one. Try to be patient and give yourself the time you need to adjust to the changes in your life. Discussing your concerns with a friend, sibling, or parent can also help you make the best of your new circumstances.

You may keep asking, "Why did this happen to me? I don't feel like I'm getting any better." But you need to try to face each day—one day at a time.

Sometimes the grief feelings become so strong that you don't think you can handle them. Or perhaps they go on for so long that normal activities don't seem important anymore. That's what happened to Brian.

Brian's father has been dead for two years. Brian has about twenty pictures of his dad along one wall in his room. His dad's hockey skates hang by the closet. He begs his mom to take him to watch the hockey team his father played on. After dinner each night, Brian listens to tapes of the family talking and joking. He loves to hear his father's voice. Brian doesn't call his friends anymore.

Brian is spending all his time remembering his dad. When he was alive, Brian's father didn't do much with him. Now Brian is dreaming about the life he wishes he'd had with his father. The way Brian is acting is not helping him overcome his grief.

It is normal for Brian to be sad. But Brian's feelings have become overwhelming. They are taking his attention away from other important areas of his life, such as family and friends.

Some teens may need help from a counselor or therapist to adjust after a death in the family.

What should you do if something like this happens to you? Talk to a friend or parent. There are also many other people who can help. Try talking to your doctor, or your pastor, priest, or rabbi. Your school counselor might suggest a support group. People in a support group all have similar problems. They meet to give each other help and support.

In the back of this book there is a list of places to call for help. Do not be afraid to seek help. Everyone goes through troubled times. If you broke your arm, you wouldn't try to fix it yourself. When you feel pain inside, you need someone who is trained to help people to deal with such problems.

Every time you grieve, you learn. Grieving helps you to appreciate all the people and things that are dear to you and that you may take for granted. That is what Marcy, Sam, and Fran learned.

Marcy had gone out with Ahmad for two years. They broke up before the prom. Missing the prom made Marcy very sad. The next day, Marcy found out she had won a basketball scholarship. Now she could afford to go to college. Ahmad had taught her to shoot baskets. She will always be glad that they knew each other.

Sam's dad taught him how to draw. They enjoyed going on hikes together and drawing pictures of the birds and animals they saw. When Sam was twelve, his dad died. Now Sam is grown up. He is a famous artist. His animal pictures are in many books. Sam says, "Every time I draw a picture, I thank Dad for what he taught me."

Fran is fourteen. She has heart disease. No one knows how much longer Fran will live. Right now she goes to school and she feels good. But this could change at any time. Fran knows she is dying. "But I try not to waste a lot of time being sad. I'd much rather spend my time enjoying life; being with friends and family and experiencing new things. It's not easy, but it's what I have to do."

Death changes your life. By grieving, you learn how to face and express your feelings about loss and change. Grieving also helps you to grow as a person. You learn to accept death as a part of life. And this acceptance can bring you the strength and the power you need to survive loss and enjoy life again.

Glossary—*Explaining New Words*

casket A box or chest used for burying a dead person.

cemetery Land reserved for burying the dead. Individual smaller sections are called plots.

cremate To change the body to ashes by burning.

depression Feelings of sadness that usually last a long time.

funeral A memorial ceremony before the burial or cremation of someone who has died.

hospice A place where dying people go to receive care.

memorial service A service in memory of someone who has died.

mourning The way we show grief or sorrow.

suicide The act of taking your own life on purpose.

support group A group of people with similar problems who get together to support and help each other.

urn A kind of vase used to keep the ashes of a cremated body.

Where to Go for Help

Call information for help in your community. Look in the yellow pages under counselors, psychologists, psychotherapy, social worker, or therapist. Find a support group to join. Ask a teacher, a doctor, or a religious leader to suggest a good therapist or place to go for help.

Compassionate Friends
P.O. Box 3696
Oak Brook, IL 60522-3696
(630) 990-0010
e-mail: tzht72a@prodigy.com
Compassionate Friends can help if your brother or sister has died.

The Dougy Center
3909 SE 52nd Avenue
P.O. Box 86852
Portland, OR 97268
(503) 775-5683
The Dougy Center provides information for teens who have lost a loved one. Contact them for support groups in your area.

The National Association of
    Social Workers
750 First Street NE
Suite 700
Washington, DC 20002
(202) 408-8600
Web site: http://www.naswdc.org

Students Against Driving
    Drunk (SADD)
P.O. Box 800
Marlboro, MA 01752
(508) 481-3568
e-mail: bc57@capecod.net

In Canada

Canadian Cancer Society
10 Alcorn Avenue
Suite 200
Toronto, ON M4V 3B1
(416) 961-7223
Web site: http://www.cancer.ca

Canadian Public Health
    Association National AIDS
    Clearinghouse
1565 Carling Avenue
Suite 400
Ottawa, ON K1Z 8R1
(613) 725-3434
Web site: http://www.cpha.ca

For Further Reading

Bode, Janet. *Death Is Hard to Live With*. New York: Bantam, Doubleday, Dell, 1993.

Gootman, Marilyn E. *When a Friend Dies: A Book for Teens About Healing and Grieving*. Minneapolis, MN: Free Spirit Publishing, 1994.

Krementz, Jill. *How It Feels When a Parent Dies*. New York: Knopf, 1996.

Kubler-Ross, Elisabeth. *On Death and Dying*. New York: Macmillan, 1993.

Kusher, Harold. *When Bad Things Happen to Good People*. New York: Schocken, 1989.

Licata, Renora. *Everything You Need to Know About Anger*. Rev. ed. New York: The Rosen Publishing Group, Inc., 1996.

Schleifer, Jay. *Everything You Need to Know About Teen Suicide*. Rev. ed. New York: The Rosen Publishing Group, Inc., 1996.

Index

A
accidental deaths, 45
AIDS, 29
anger, 6, 10, 12, 37, 38, 43

C
casket, 50
cemetery, 52
changes, adjusting to, 38–39,
    56–57
cremation, 52–53

D
death
    definition of, 22
    of someone young, 41–43
depression, 13, 47, 48
disbelief (about a death), 34
divorce, 17, 56
drugs, turning to, 19

F
fear, 13, 38
    of death, 25, 27
friend, death of, 11, 41–42

funeral, 49, 50
    customs, 52
funeral homes, 50–52

G
grief
    causes of, 9
    definition of, 6
    recovering from, 55–59
    "work," 17
guilt, 12, 37, 38, 46

H
home, death at, 22, 27
hospice, 27

J
jealousy, 37

L
longing, 12

M
memorial services, 50
memories (of a loved one), 36, 43
mourning, 50–52

P

parent, death of, 24, 33–39, 56, 57

pet, death of, 9, 10, 15–16, 25

R

relative, death of, 10, 25–26, 29–32

relief (after death), 30

religion, 27, 52

S

sadness, 12, 34, 38, 48, 55, 59

shiva, 52

shock, 11, 34, 37, 45

sudden deaths, 46–48

suicide, 46–48

support groups, 58

sympathy, showing, 53

V

violent death, 48

W

wake, 52

worry, 33–34, 38, 42

About the Author

Karen Spies was an elementary school teacher and vice principal before embarking on a second career in publishing. She has written several books for young people.

Acknowledgments and Photo Credits

Photographs by Barbara Kirk

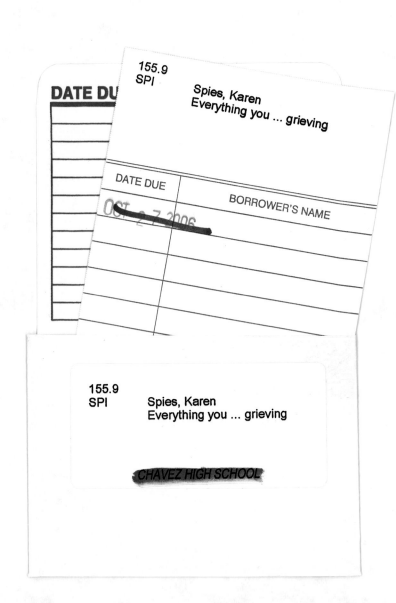